101 Uses

Even Duct tape can't fix stupid
But it can muffle the sound!

Muhammad Naveed
Mendon Cottage Books

JD-Biz Publishing

Disclaimer

The information is this book is provided for informational purposes only. It is not intended to be used and medical advice or a substitute for proper medical treatment by a qualified health care provider. The information is believed to be accurate as presented based on research by the author.

The contents have not been evaluated by the U.S. Food and Drug Administration or any other Government or Health Organization and the contents in this book are not to be used to treat cure or prevent disease.

The author or publisher is not responsible for the use or safety of any diet, procedure or treatment mentioned in this book. The author or publisher is not responsible for errors or omissions that may exist.

Warning

The Book is for informational purposes only and should not be taken too seriously. It is from the twisted mind of the author.

Our books are available at

1. Amazon.com
2. Barnes and Noble
3. Itunes
4. Kobo
5. Smashwords
6. Google Play Books

Table of Contents

Introduction

A very commonly used adhesive or sticky medium used for several purposes is called duct tape. It is often referred to as duck-tape as well. In many instances, this tape is coated with polyethylene material and has a cloth or scrim backing. Duct tape is easily available in the market at very cheap rates. There are various duct tape varieties that you can choose from. It is mostly available in grey and black shades but other colors can also be made to order. It is a multipurpose tool that can come handy in many different types of situations and scenarios. Although there can be an infinite number of utilities for duct tape, some of them are provided below:

Babysitting Your Little Sister

Just kidding but you can have a lot of fun with duct tape.

Replacement of Shoe Laces

Duct tape can be used for the replacement of shoe laces. If you do not have shoes laces and want to secure your shoes so that they do not fall off when you walk, then duct tape is best thing that can hold the grip together. It helps close the flaps of the shoes and keep the foot tightly inside the shoes even without any shoes laces.

Secure Your Car Keys

There are many people who often lose their car keys and spend lots of time searching for them, or want a hidden key. A good idea to keep these car keys secure is to stick them to the bottom of the car with duct tape. This will ensure that your car keys are safely kept and at the time of need they can simply be removed from the bottom and used to start your car.

Hanging Pictures

Decorating the walls of your room with different types of posters and pictures has been a very long standing tradition. Whether the building is your home or office posters of various kinds are pasted on the walls using duct tape. This is an easy and cheap method of decorating your building walls. Sometimes these posters may be advertisements for any special product or service.

Can Be Used As a Bookmark

If you are fond reading then you must feel the need for a bookmark to remember the page that you left in the previous session of reading. Duct tape can be used for this purpose by folding it inside out and keeping in in between the pages as a bookmark.

As A Vinyl Patch

Duct tape is an excellent material to be used as a patching tool for different forms of vinyl products and surfaces. It offers a secure cover for any type of hole or crack provided it is not very large.

Fix a Car Light

A broken tail-light in your vehicle can be considered a traffic rule violation in many parts of the world. Therefore in order to remove the defect and keep the expense as low as possible using duct tape is a great medium for fixing the tail-light of your vehicle until you can replace it.

Duct Tape as an Art Medium

Duct tape can be used to create different types of arts and crafts. It is adhesive in nature and can be used to stick together various arts and craft materials.

Holding Wigs in Place

Mannequins are well decorated with not only clothes and apparel but also wigs on their heads. Duct tape can be used a great medium for sticking their wigs on their heads.

Patching Shoes

If you have an urgent meeting and you end up breaking your shoe or notice a hole in it, then the best possible solution for an urgent fix is to use duct tape to patch it up. It is cheap and cost effective as well.

Can Be Used As a Waist Band or Belt

If you have loose trousers and pants that keep slipping of your waist, then you can use duct tape to keep them tight and gripped. The duct tape can be used to make a great belt, which will not let the trousers slip off your waist.

Patching Up a Pool Puncture

Rubber and inflated swimming pools are commonly used in the summers. Every house with a kid seems to have one of these pools in their front lawn. However due to their delicate build, they are very much prone to punctures. For an urgent fix, duct tape can be used to patch up the hole in the swimming pool and fill it up with water.

Holding the Bumper in Place

Sometimes through small hits and kicks the bumper of your car can be easily knocked off. To keep it up in the right position you can use duct tape to stick it back up. It is a cheap and easy way of repairing your car bumper.

Fixing Books

Book covers and binding often get lose or torn due to excessive utilization and reading or some other misuse of the book. Duct tape is the perfect solution of fixing the binding and cover of the book.

As a Line Marker

During a sporting event that has to be arranged in an open field, lines need to be drawn. Duct tape is used to mark these lines and keep them straight.

Muting a Person

Duct tape when stuck on the mouth of a person can keep him mute for several hours if not removed. You can do this to a number of people by force.

Makeshift Money Wallet

If you want to keep your money safe without a wallet you can use some paper and duct tape and secure it together to form an envelope or wallet.

Tying Hands Together

Duct tape can be used as hand cuffs for tying the hands of a person together. This way he will not be able to use his hands until the duct tape is removed.

Repairing Spilt Soles in Shoes

If the sole of your shoes is losing its adhesiveness and splitting up at the toe, you can use duct tape to keep it together and moving swiftly and easily. This is a very quick and easy way to fix your damaged shoe if you have less time and no money at all.

As a Bumper Sticker

Duct tape can be used in combination with a sharpie to make an amazing bumper sticker for your vehicle. This is a very genuine and creative way of making a bumper sticker.

Clothing Line

Sometimes when you wash your clothes in a camping site or at a hotel you can't find a clothing line to put them on. Duct tape can be used to erect a clothing line for drying your washed laundry. The duct tape itself acts as the clothes line.

Bicycle Streamers

We all like to decorate and make our bicycle attractive and colorful. Duct tape can be used for this purpose as well. Colorful and smooth streamers can be created using duct tape and hanging them on to the handles of the bicycle. They will enhance the outlook of the bicycle.

Utility Pockets

There are a number of times where we lose our important documents in our own houses. We forget where we have kept them and are unable to find them when they are needed. Duct tape and cardboard paper can be used to create small pouches or pockets on the doors of our room or office to keep important documents and other important stuff.

Costume for Halloween or a Fancy Dress Party

If you are looking for a creative and unique idea for a costume party or Halloween night then think no more. Duct tape wrapped around your entire body to create a mummy costume is not only creative and unique it is also very cheap to make.

Repairing Hoses

If you have broken hoses in your home or office, then duct tape can provide the most quick and easy remedy to fix these hoses temporarily.

Sticking Stuff on Lockers

As students we all stuck pictures and posters of our favorite celebrities, sportsman and friends on our locker walls and doors. Duct tape can be used for this purpose as well.

Biore Strip

Duct tape can be used as a Biore strip to clean the pores on your face as well. Have a treatment at home.

Locking the Door

If you want to lock a door or someone inside a room you can use duct tape to seal the hinges and cracks of the door. Lots of duct tape may be required but it sure will help keep the door locked for some time.

Seat Cover Repairs

The seat covers of your car or any other vehicles are prone to the most wear and tear over a period of time. Sometimes small holes will appear due to some pointed object or a cigarette burn. Duct tape may be used to patch up such holes or damages in the seat covers.

Sticking Up of Basketball Hoop

If you are fond of playing basketball even in your own bedroom then you need to have a basketball hoop as well. Duct tape can be used to stick the ring on to your door or wall easily.

Tent Holes Repair

Camping cannot be complete without a tent. If you have a hole in your tent it can be a problem if there is rain or wind. Duct tape can be used to patch up such holes in you camping tent and save you a lot of pain and hassle. So next time you go camping do not forget to take a duct tape roll which can be very handy.

Fixing Blinds

Windows are very delicate and can be broken or damaged by a single jerk or a little force. To keep them functional and in position we can repair them by using duct tape. It is easy and light and does not require a lot of hassle to fix.

Muzzle

Duct tape can be used to create a muzzle.

Waterproof Protection

When working in the kitchen or maybe in your garden shed you need to have an apron that can keep the stains away from your clothes. This apron should be waterproof so that your clothes are protected from water and stains. Sticking duct tape all over the apron can make the material of the apron water resistant and will be easily cleaned with a single wipe or sweep.

Repairing A PVC Pipe

Plastic or PVC pipes are used for various purposes in a building. But they are very much prone to breakage or cracks. These cracks and holes can be patched using duct tape as a fixing medium.

De-Cluttering Wires

We use a number of electric appliances in our houses and offices. Their wires remain spread across the room and can be a hazard not only for little children but also for adults. People can fumble and trip on these wires causing severe damages. You can use duct tape to stick these wires together and stick them to the floor firmly.

As A Bandage

If you are in a remote location and do not have the access to a first aid box, then duct tape can be used to create a band aid and keep your small cuts and wounds covered. This will protect them from dust and germs.

Repairing Door Hinges

If the hinges of your cabinet door are broken or lose, you can use duct tape to tighten it and stick it together. This will allow easy and functional movement of the cabinet doors.

Repairing Holes in Clothing

Just like your shoes, you may encounter a hole or damage in your clothes at anytime and anywhere. A small jerk with a pointed objected can badly tear your clothes. To keep them together or to repair them immediately without any hassle you can use duct tape.

Fixing a Vacuum Cleaner

If the hose of your vacuum cleaner is cracked or broken or its sack has a hole in it, then duct tape can be used to repair its various damages. This is a quick and easy solution to the problem.

Sticking Boots with Skis

If the binding of your ski boots is broken or damaged you can easily use duct tape to keep them stuck on the skis. Skiing is a tough activity and if the boots are lose or jerky it can cause a fatal accident as well. So to avoid any such incidents or mishaps it is advised to use duct tape as a sticking agent.

Repairing Work Gloves

Work gloves are an essential requirement of many professions or jobs. Working without gloves is not recommended at all. If your work gloves become damaged or torn during an activity you can repair them by using duct tape. This useful tape can be used for filling in of cracks and patching up of holes.

Wristband

Duct tape can be used as a fashion accessory to make various types of wristbands and bangles. It can be also be used as a utility band for writing pertinent information on the band or as an identification band.

Cd Case

If you have a CD that is without a case or cover it is sure to get damaged or scratched. To keep it safely and protected you need to have a CD cover. Duct tape and paper can be used to create a CD cover for its protection. You can also label the name of the CD for identification.

Repairing Broken Windows

If your window glass is broken or cracked it can cause a lot of discomfort. It not only allows winds to enter the room but also dust and other particles. To keep them safely secure and closed you can use duct tape to fill them up. Whole broken windows can also be covered up by using duct tape on the entire portion.

Realistic Props

Duct tape can be used to create real looking props for various purposes.

Mouse Trap

Duct tape and a few other materials can be used to create an effective mouse trap.

Make a Wallet Chain

A wallet is a valuable item that you keep with you to protect your money. However there are a number of pick pockets around who can steal your wallet. You also have the risk of losing your wallet if it accidentally falls down from your pocket. Duct tape can be used to create a wallet chain that sticks with your pocket. This makes it difficult for any pick pocket to take your wallet and it is not easily lost through falling down.

Sticking a Guitar Strap

The purpose of a guitar strap is to hold the guitar in the right position and also to remain comfortable. During a performance if this strap breaks off it can cause some serious discomfort especially if you are going to stand up while playing the guitar. Duct tape can be used to stick this strap on the guitar and hold it in place securely.

Headband

Duct tape can be used to create a stylish headband to meet your fashion needs. It can also be used to write down slogans or identification information.

Suspenders

If your pants or trousers are larger than your waist then they will keep falling off until you secure them with a belt of suspenders. The duct tape can be used as suspenders under your coat or jacket. It can stick on to your belt of the pants and keep it tightly pulled up on to your shoulders just like a suspender.

Broken Leg

If you are in a remote location or camping or hiking and you or any of your friends get a broken leg, you will need to attach it with a splint to keep it straight. For this purpose a duct tape is the best possible medium for keeping the splint attached with the broken leg.

Sealing Snack Bags

While eating chips and other crispy snacks some might be left in the bag. If you let the bags stay open for long periods of time the chips will become soggy, soft or stale. To retain the crispiness of the snack or chips you must re seal the bag. Duct tape can be used to close the bag again and reopen it to experience the same crispiness of the chips in the future.

Repairing of Ski Gloves

If the seams of your ski gloves become lose or broken, skiing can be not only uncomfortable but also dangerous. So you must repair them immediately. Duct tape is the best possible medium that can help you repair the ski gloves on an urgent basis without much hassle.

Repair a Boat or Canoe

Those of you who are fond of rowing and boating must have encountered a small hole in your boat or canoe at one time or another. This can be patched up urgently using a small piece of duct tape.

Spike and Cleats

Duct tape may be used for keeping the spikes attached to the cleats. Is it not interesting? Enjoy!

Keeping the Car Door Closed

For any purpose or reason you may require closing a car door so that no one can open it. For this purpose too you can seal it with duct tape. Although a lot of duct tape may be required the need will be fulfilled.

Fly Catcher

The duct tape can be used to stick the fly-paper onto the fly prone surface. It can itself be used as fly paper if the sticky side remains on the top.

Creating Vinyl Floors

You can paste layers of duct tape on the floor to create a vinyl look on your flooring. It will be easy to clean and wipe off. You will also not be worried about staining the floor with various elements.

Small Patch for Fish Tanks

Anyone with a fish as a pet must also have a fish tank. What if your tank suddenly got a crack or hole in it? How would you keep the fish alive without water? Simply use duct tape to patch the crack or hole of the fish tank. It is easy and convenient and provides a good solution but only for a short time.

Gift Wrapping

All of us give gifts on different occasions. These gifts are mostly wrapped up in decorative paper to make them more attractive. Duct tape makes gift wrapping a breeze as it can be used to hold the paper together. It is a great medium without which gift wrapping can be very difficult.

Blister Repairs

If you end up with any kind of blister on your foot then you can use duct tape to apply to the blister and create a protective barrier between the blister and your footwear.

Writing on Vehicles

Writing on vehicles may be necessary for some corporate or professional reasons. Or you may like to write something to expression your thoughts or views. This writing can be done with the help of duct tape. It will stick easily and can also be removed when required.

Holding In a Battery

Sometimes the cover of the battery compartment of a number of battery operated toys and remote controls gets lost. This makes the batteries become lose and fall out of the compartment very frequently. To keep the batteries secure and covered you can use duct tape for sealing the compartment.

Tool Belts

When you are repairing or working on various types of crafts or DIY projects you need to have a tool belt. This tool belt can be created using duct tape around your waist.

Covering a Book

If you do not like the cover of a book or it is too delicate to be damaged you can cover it yourself with some decorative ideas. Duct tape can be used for facilitating and sticking the decorative cover of the book.

Use It As a Rope

In many situations you may require the need of a rope. But it is not always possible that the rope is immediately available. In such situations the duct tape can come in very handy. Twisting together few strands of duct tape can lead to the creation of a great rope. It will be durable as well as strong.

Securing Vehicle Bumper

The bumper of a vehicle is prone to the largest number of accidental risks. Little hits from the back or front can cause a large number of scratches and breakages on the bumper. For this reason you need to have some extra protection on it. This can be provided using several layers of duct tape to cover the bumper.

Hold Pens and Pencils Together

At home or at the office for example, you may easily lose your pencils and pens. To keep them secure and close by, you can use duct tape. They can be stuck together using duct tape all around them.

Napkin Rings

Sometimes you may not be able to locate your best utensils or tools when you absolutely need them. For example, when you have dinner party and you are unable to find your best napkin rings you can use duct tape to hold napkins together in a particular shape selected by you.

Window Covering

For sunny summer days when there is excessive sunlight and heat flowing in through the windows, you may sometimes feel like covering the windows up completely. In such situations where you may not have curtains, you can use duct tape to stick black paper on the windows to block the sunlight.

Reaching Small Objects

Several times in our lives we may accidentally drop our small objects in tight or small areas. It becomes very difficult to reach out to such small objects and take them out. Duct tape hanging from a stick or rod can be used effectively. The object may stick to the duct tape and can be easily retrieved.

Picture Framing

Duct tape can be very easily used to make picture frames. Coloring the duct tape can create a number of DIY framing projects and also add a bit of decoration to your room.

Making a Hat

You can use duct tape and paper to create a fantastic hat for your special parties and occasions. It is also offers great amusement for kids playing the role of a cowboy or sheriff.

Repairing Car Trims

Duct tape is used widely for repair and maintenance of trims on vehicles. Don't forget to have this repairing tool in your car's tool box.

Repairing Furniture or Upholstery

If you break any of your furniture pieces or get a hole or rip in the upholstery of your furniture, it can make a very bad impression on guests. You can utilize duct tape for an immediate solution. Simply use the duct tape to patch up the holes or damages if any.

Lint Removal

Lint accumulation is a common problem that appears after wearing clothing for few days. It mostly occurs on warm clothes like jersey, coats and sweaters. One of the easiest and cheapest ways to remove lint on clothes is by using duct tape. Stick it on the portion of lint you want to remove and pull it back up. This will remove the lint particles as well.

Repair Small Toys

If you have kids then there must be a number of toys in your house. Kids play with toys and break them often. Duct tape is a very useful medium to help repair such small toys so that your kids remain happy.

Velcro Replacement

Duct tape can be used in place of Velcro or if the Velcro is worn out and has lost its stickiness.

Repairing Holes in a Convertible Roof

If on a rainy day you find out that there is a hole in your convertible or roof of a jeep, you can use duct tape to patch up this hole in a very cheap and effective manner.

Broken Kitchen Bowls

If you have cracked bowls in your kitchen they can be mended using a duct tape. It will help you maintaining your budget.

Laptop Protector for Laptop

You can apply duct tape on the back of your laptop to keep it protected from scratches and small hits.

Purse Strap

If the strap of your handbag or purse suddenly breaks you can use twisted lines of duct tape to make a strap.

Repairing Socks

If you have unfortunately just noticed a hole in your sock you will naturally be worried about how to hide it. The best and easiest way to repair holes in your socks is by using duct tape.

Making a Ball

If you feel like playing with a ball or your kid wants a ball and you do not have one, how can you quickly find a ball? It is pretty easy. Just take duct tape and wrap in around a ball of paper. Apply several layers to make the ball a little heavy and round to play.

Toilet Seat Repairs

One of the common problems in houses and offices is a broken or cracked toilet seat. A quick way of fixing this problem is using duct tape to repair it.

Repairing of a Shower Curtain

Shower curtains are usually made up of materials that can be easily torn. Especially if you have kids, a shower curtain can be at risk of being damaged when children constantly pull on it while getting in and out of the bath. Duct tape can be used easily to stick the shower curtain together and repair it.

Piñata

If you are looking forward to making a piñata for a birthday party then you can use lots of paper and duct tape to hold it together.

Duct Joints

Many times duct tape might be useful in joining together various ducts. But this is only a temporary solution.

Repairing File Covers

Many times offices files covers get torn due to excessive usage or inappropriate storage of files. Duct tape is the best possible solution for repairing the file covers and keeping them safe for longer periods of time.

Mend a Carpet

If your carpet gets ripped or torn from one side it can be dangerous and depreciate the appearance of your room and its decor. For this purpose you can repair the ends safely using duct tape as a good adhesive.

Fixing Broken Decoration Pieces

If you live with kids, then your vases and other decorations are nowhere near safe. They can fall and break thanks to the horseplay in which young ones often engage. So you will definitely need to have duct tape around to mend and repair your small breakable items.

Holding Up Socks

If socks are worn for long periods of time they may deteriorate quickly. The elastic grip on the top of the socks becomes old and loose and causes them to slip down your legs again and again. To keep them tightly gripped to the legs you can use duct tape.

Create Disk Labels

If you are tired of mixing up your CDs and being unable to find the right one at the right time then you need to have labels on them. You can use paper and duct tape to make small disk labels that will free you from the big hassle of finding your favorite music.

Sealing Letters and Envelopes

Duct tape can be used to seal envelopes, holding letters and other important documents in them.

Make a Leash

Duct tape is strong and unbreakable. It can be twisted around as a rope and then used as a leash for your small pets.

Making Footwear Waterproof

If you have to walk in the rain or snow your shoes often get wet. Duct tape can be used to make shoes waterproof.

Wire Taping

When joining and connection wires we need to splice them. Duct tape is used to join them together afterwards.

Repairing Tires and Tubes

Small holes in tubes and tires can be repaired temporarily using duct tape. Using this repair you can easily reach to a tire shop.

Lighting

While putting up decorative lights on various occasions, especially Christmas, duct tape can be a very useful medium.

Broken Mirrors

If you have broken your rear view or side view mirror it can be easily repaired using duct tape.

Shutting Up Your Mother-In-Law

You can shut the mouth of your talkative mother-in-law using duct tape, or other annoying people. This may get you in trouble and could cause you to experience many forms of torture that can come from duct tape.

Even Duct tape can't fix stupid
But it can muffle the sound

Thus we see that there are a wide range of activities and utilities that can be achieved using duct tape. Ranging from broken objects, making connections, using it for arts and crafts and even as a tool to shut the mouths of chatter boxes, the list of uses for duct tape can go on and on. There is no finite number of utilities for duct tape. Due to its strong make and type duct tape is very durable and is water resistant as well. Initially developed for defense related purposes, duct tape has become a very common household commodity these days. It is present in almost every house of the world.

With its multi-purpose properties and utilities people get a great value for the amount of money that they spend on buying a roll of duct tape. So next time you decide to go shopping make sure that you buy a roll of duct tape and keep it with you at all times. You never know when it can become handy. The above 101 uses for duct tape must have given you a number of new ideas on how to use this wonderful 20th century invention.

Author Bio

Author Name Muhammad Naveed

Muhammad Naveed is currently engaged in craft consultancy, particularly, Handloom Weaving, Block Printing and Natural Dyes. He completed his Masters in Computer Sciences and Political Science, and in addition to providing consultancy and training, he is writing books and web content on various topics. He has written numerous books, articles, case studies, reports and essays on craft, IT and academic related niches. He loves sharing his ideas and knowledge with others.

Check out some of the other JD-Biz Publishing books

Gardening Series on Amazon

Health Learning Series

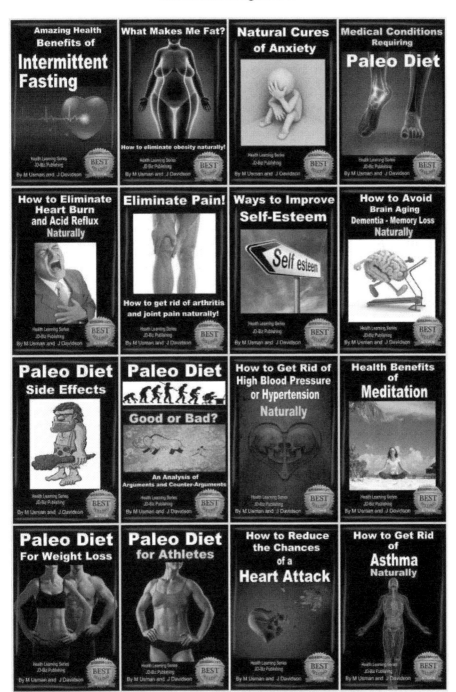

Amazing Animal Book Series

Chinchillas | Beavers | Snakes | Dolphins | Wolves | Walruses
Polar Bears | Turtles | Bees | Frogs | Horses | Monkeys
Dinosaurs | Sharks | Whales | Spiders | Big Cats | Big Mammals of Yellowstone
Animals of Australia | Sasquatch - Yeti Abominable Snowman Bigfoot | Giant Panda Bears | Kittens | Komodo Dragons | Lady Bugs
Animals of North America | Meerkats | Birds of North America | Penguins | Hamsters | Elephants

Learn To Draw Series

How to Build and Plan Books

Entrepreneur Book Series

Our books are available at

1. Amazon.com

2. Barnes and Noble

3. Itunes

4. Kobo

5. Smashwords

6. Google Play Books

Publisher

JD-Biz Corp

P O Box 374

Mendon, Utah 84325

http://www.jd-biz.com/

Mendon Cottage Books

P O Box 374, Mendon Utah 84325

Made in United States
Orlando, FL
16 December 2024

55922943R00026